THIS BOOK BELONGS TO

_____

_____

_____

_____

DABBING UNICORN

DABBING OWL

DABBING COW

Dabbing Animal

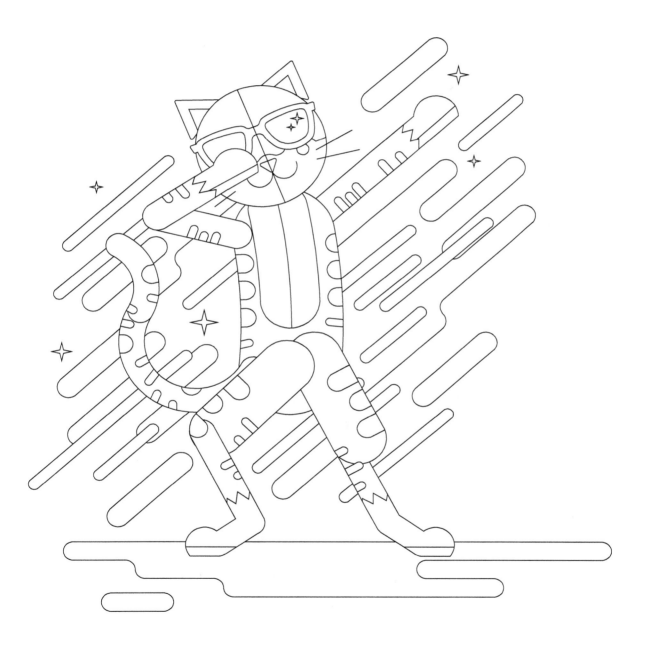

DABBING RABBIT

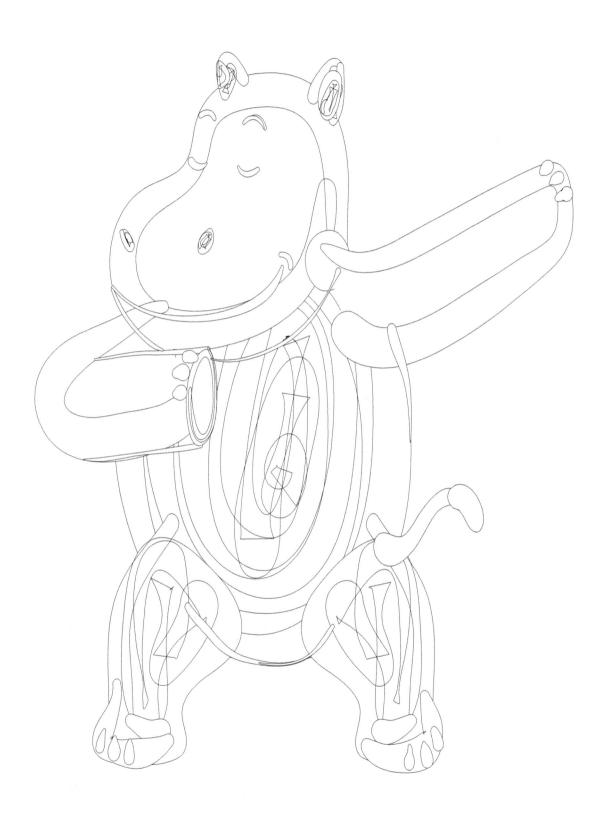

www.ingramcontent.com/pod-product-compliance
Lightning Source LLC
Chambersburg PA
CBHW080602060326
40689CB00021B/4908